To all the good children who ate
their broccoli tonight

The Coyote Rings the Wrong Bell

A Mexican Folktale

Illustrated by Francisco X. Mora

CHILDRENS PRESS ®
CHICAGO

Adventures in Storytelling

Dear Parents and Teachers,

Adventures in Storytelling Books have been designed to delight storytellers of all ages and to make world literature available to non-readers as well as to those who speak English as a second language. The wordless format and accompanying audiocassette make it possible for both readers and nonreaders who are unacquainted with a specific ethnic folktale to use either the visual or the audio portion as an aid in understanding the story.

For additional reference the complete story text is printed in the back of the book, and post-story activities are suggested for those who enjoy more participation.

The history of storytelling

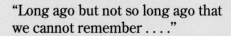

"Once upon a time . . . ."

"Long ago but not so long ago that we cannot remember . . . ."

"In the grey, grey beginnings of the world . . . ."

"And it came to pass, more years ago than I can tell you . . . ."

These are magic words. They open kingdoms and countries beyond our personal experiences and make the impossible possible and the miraculous, if not commonplace, at least not unexpected.

For hundreds of years people have been telling stories. You do it every day, every time you say, "You'll never believe what happened to me yesterday"; or "You know, something like that happened to my grandmother, but according to her, it went something like this . . . ."

Before video recorders, tape recorders, television, and radio, there was storytelling. It was the vehicle through which every culture remembered its past and kept alive its heritage. It was the way people explained life, shared events, and entertained themselves around the fire on dark, lonely nights. The stories they told evoked awe and respect for tradition, ritual, wisdom, and power; transmitted cultural taboos and teachings from generation to generation; and made people laugh at the foolishness in life or cry when confronted by life's tragedies.

As every culture had its stories, so too did each have its storytellers. In Africa they were called griots; in Ireland, seanachies; in France, troubadours; and in the majority of small towns and villages around the world they were simply known as the gifted. Often their stories were hundreds of years old. Some of them were told exactly as they had been told for centuries; others were changed often to reflect people's interests and where and how they lived.

With the coming of the printing press and the availability of printed texts, the traditional storyteller began to disappear — not altogether and not everywhere, however. There were pockets in the world where stories were kept alive by those who remembered them and believed in them. Although not traditional storytellers, these people continued to pass down folktales, even though the need for formal, professional storytelling was fading.

In the nineteenth century, the Grimm brothers made the folktale fashionable, and for the first time collections of tales from many countries became popular. Story collections by Andrew Lang, Joseph Jacobs, and Charles Perrault became the rage, with one important difference: these stories were written down to be read, not told aloud to be heard.

As the nineteenth century gave way to the twentieth, there was a revival of interest in storytelling. Spearheaded by children's librarians and schoolteachers, a new kind of storytelling evolved — one that was aimed specifically at children and connected to literature and reading. The form of literature most chosen by these librarians and teachers was the traditional folktale.

During this time prominent educator May Hill Arbuthnot wrote that children were a natural audience for folktales because the qualities found in these tales were those to which children normally responded in stories: brisk action, humor, and an appeal to a sense of justice. Later, folklorist Max Luthi supported this theory. He called the folktale a fundamental building block, an outstanding aid in child development, and the archetypal form of literature that lays the groundwork for all literature.

By the middle of the twentieth century, storytelling was seen as a way of exposing children to literature that they would not discover by themselves and of making written language accessible to those who could not read it by themselves. Storytelling became a method of promoting an understanding of other cultures and a means of strengthening the cultural awareness of the listening group; a way of creating that community of listeners that evolves when a diverse group listens to a tale well-told.

Many of these same reasons for storytelling are valid today — perhaps even more relevant than they were nearly one hundred years ago. Current research confirms what librarians and teachers have known all along — that storytelling provides a practical, effective, and enjoyable way to introduce children to literature while fostering a love of reading. It connects the child to the story and the book. Through storytelling, great literature (the classics, poetry, traditional folktales) comes alive; children learn to love language and experience the beauty of the spoken word, often before they master those words by reading them themselves.

Without exception, all cultures have accumulated a body of folktales that represent their history, beliefs, and language. Yet, while each culture's folktales are unique, they also are connected to the folktales of other cultures through the universality of themes contained within them. Some of the most common themes appearing in folktales around the world deal with good overcoming evil; the clever outwitting the strong; and happiness being the reward for kindness to strangers, the elderly, and the less fortunate. We hear these themes repeated in stories from quaint Irish villages along the Atlantic coast to tiny communities spread throughout the African veldt and from cities and towns of the industrialized Americas to the magnificent palaces of the emperors of China and Japan. It is these similarities that are fascinating; that help us to transcend the barriers of language, politics, custom, and religion; and that bind us together as "the folk" in folktales.

Using wordless picture books and audiocassettes

Every child is a natural storyteller. Children begin telling stories almost as soon as they learn to speak. The need to share what they experience and how they perceive life prompts them to organize their thoughts and express themselves in a way others will under-stand. But storytelling goes beyond the everyday need to communicate. Beyond the useful, storytelling can be developed into a skill that entertains and teaches. Using wordless picture books and audiocassettes aids in this process.

When children hear a story told, they are learning much about language, story structure, plot development, words, and the development of a "sense of story." Wordless books encourage readers to focus on pictures for the story line and the sequence of events, which builds children's visual skills. In time, the "visually literate" child will find it easier to develop verbal and written skills.

Because a wordless folktale book is not restricted by reading ability or educational level, it can be used as a tool in helping children and adults, both English and non-English speakers, as well as readers and nonreaders to understand or retell a story from their own rich, ethnic perspective. Listening to folktales told on an audiocassette or in person offers another advantage; it allows the listener, who may be restricted by reading limitations, to enjoy literature, learn about other cultures, and develop essential prereading skills. Furthermore, it gives them confidence to retell stories on their own and motivates them to learn to read them.

Something special happens when you tell a story; something special happens when you hear a story well-told. Storytelling is a unique, entertaining, and powerful art form, one that creates an intimate bond between storyteller and listener, past and present. To take a story and give it a new voice is an exhilarating experience; to watch someone else take that same story and make it his or her own is another.

Janice M. Del Negro
Children's Services
The Chicago Public Library

The following tale is a delightful Mexican fable about two favorite animals — the hare and the coyote. After being caught by a hungry coyote, the clever hare fools his captor into letting him go free.

Story text

One day Señor Rabbit decided to take a siesta after having his midday meal. He curled up under a big shade tree and was soon fast asleep.

Well, not more than five minutes after he had begun dozing, Señor Coyote came by. As soon as he spied the rabbit, his mouth began to water, for he was very hungry. Señor Coyote hadn't eaten for days!

So he silently crept up to the tree, and then pounced squarely on top of the sleeping rabbit, who awoke with a start.

"Ah, ha!" said Señor Coyote, "I've got you now!" And he began to lick his lips.

Señor Rabbit was so surprised that he could do nothing but breathe hard.

"Mmmm," said the coyote, poking his paws at Señor Rabbit's stomach, "you feel nice and fat. You must have just had a big lunch! You'll make a fine lunch for me!"

By now, the rabbit had gathered his wits.

"Oh, yes," he said, "I did have a very good lunch. But, you know, I'm very old, and very dry, and very tough. I don't mind if you eat me because I'm not going to live much longer anyway. But Señor Coyote, would you grant me one last favor?"

"Huh? A favor? What favor?"

"Well, you see, I'm supposed to ring the recess bell for all the juicy, tender, little hares in the schoolhouse over there," replied Señor Rabbit. "It's the job they give to us old, dry, tough-meated rabbits."

The coyote's ears perked up. "Did you say juicy and tender little hares?"

"Oh, yes, that's what I said. Juicy and tender."

"And where is the bell?"

Señor Rabbit pointed to a hornet's nest in the branches above. "See, there it is. I shake the tree very hard, and the bell rings."

"And the juicy, tender, little hares come out whenever you ring the bell?"

"Every time."

"Mmmm. Well, suddenly I'm not so hungry," said Señor Coyote, as he jumped off Señor Rabbit. "So I won't eat you."

"You must be very stiff from my holding you down. Why don't you go for a little walk and shake the stiffness from your bones? I'll ring the bell for you."

"Well, no. I thank you for offering, brother Coyote. But it's a very important job. I must do it myself."

"Oh, please let me do it. I feel badly about jumping on you that way and frightening you. It would make me feel so much better if I could do a favor for you as amends. I would like to do this for you, Señor Rabbit."

"Well, if you insist. OK! But you must wait for the right time—when the sun reaches the top of the trees over there on the hill."

"Oh, I promise."

"And be sure to shake the tree violently. Otherwise the juicy, tender, little hares won't hear the bell."

"Si, I promise. Violently."

So Señor Rabbit hopped away, chuckling to himself all the way home.

As soon as he was out of sight, Señor Coyote, his mouth watering, began shaking the tree with all his might—shaking it so hard that the hornet's nest fell on his head.

Suddenly, the air was filled with hundreds of angry hornets, buzzing loudly and stinging Señor Coyote all over his body.

To escape, he ran to a nearby pond and jumped in, but not before he was covered with stings.

After the hornets flew away, Señor Coyote got out of the pond and looked at his reflection in the water.

"Aeeii!" he cried, looking at the long stingers sticking out of his body. "I look like a porcupine! I only wanted juicy, tender little hares, not porcupine hairs!"

Project Editor: Alice Flanagan
Design and Electronic Page Composition: Biner Design
Engraver: Liberty Photoengravers

About the storyteller

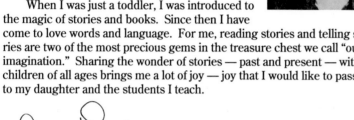

My name is Anamarie Garcia. I am the storyteller you hear on the tape recording of *The Coyote Rings the Wrong Bell*. I live in Arizona where I am a theatre arts teacher, storyteller, puppeteer, actress, director, and creative drama specialist. My most demanding roles, however, are as mother to my four year-old daughter, Rachel, and wife to my husband, Joe.

When I was just a toddler, I was introduced to the magic of stories and books. Since then I have come to love words and language. For me, reading stories and telling stories are two of the most precious gems in the treasure chest we call "our imagination." Sharing the wonder of stories — past and present — with children of all ages brings me a lot of joy — joy that I would like to pass on to my daughter and the students I teach.

About the illustrator

Born in Mexico City in 1952, Francisco Mora became an art student at an early age. During his formative years, he studied traditional and contemporary art with the most influential Mexican artists of his time and also studied in Europe and the United States.

Today, Mr. Mora is quickly becoming one of the country's most important contemporary Latin American painters.

In his paintings, Francisco speaks through whimsical animals native to Mexico. His art possesses an almost allegorical quality, conveying an ability to speak through the images that convey bits and pieces of Mexican heritage.

Referring to himself and his work, Francisco says, "There was a time when I had grandiose dreams, but then I didn't have a language for my own expression. When I found that language, I knew that I could be talking forever."

Storytelling activities

Storytelling provides a wonderful opportunity to share information, feelings, and a love of books with children. Some of the following activities may be helpful in making this possible:

- Ask children to retell the story. This will help you measure their comprehension and interact with them through quiet conversation.

- Have paper and magic markers or crayons available so children can draw the story. You might ask them to draw a picture of one of the characters in the book or make a story map (a series of drawings reflecting the sequence of story events).

- Ask children to tell the story from different points of view. Have them retell the story several times — each time basing it on the viewpoint of a different character.

More about storytelling and folktales

If you'd like to read more about storytelling or other Mexican folktales, check out some of the following books from your local library:

Breneman, Lucille N. and Bren. *Once Upon a Time: A Storytelling Handbook*. Chicago: Nelson-Hall, 1983.

Sierra, Judy. *Twice Upon a Time: Stories to Tell, Retell, Act Out and Write About*. New York: H. W. Wilson, 1989.

Campbell, Camilla. *Star Mountain and other Legends of Mexico*. New York: McGraw Hill, 1968.

Lyons, Grant. *Tales That People Tell in Mexico*. New York: J. Messner, 1972.

Library of Congress Cataloging-in-Publication Data

Mora, Francisco X.

    The coyote rings the wrong bell: A Mexican folktale / illustrated by Francisco X. Mora.

       p. cm. — (Adventures in storytelling)

    Summary: After being caught by a hungry coyote, a clever hare fools his captor into letting him go free. A list for adults of storytelling activites is included.

      ISBN 0-516-05136-9

      [1. Folklore—Mexico.] I. Title. II. Series.

PZ8.1.M79Co 1991

398.2—dc20   91-13163

[E]   CIP
                                            AC

Copyright © 1991 by Childrens Press ®, Inc.
All rights reserved. Published simultaneously in Canada.
Printed in the United States of America.
1 2 3 4 5 6 7 8 9 10 R 99 98 97 96 95 94 93 92 91 90